RADIANCE

RADIANCE

Emanuel Xavier

REBEL SATORI PRESS
New Orleans, LA • Bar Harbor, ME

Author Photo: Brian Berger
Book Design: Sven Davisson

ISBN: 978-1-60864-121-5

Rebel Satori Press
Bar Harbor, ME

Library of Congress Cataloging-in-Publication Data

Names: Xavier, Emanuel, author.
Title: Radiance / Emanuel Xavier.
Description: New Orleans : Rebel Satori Press, [2016]
Identifiers: LCCN 2016013826 (print) | LCCN 2016014013 (ebook) | ISBN
9781608641215 (pbk.) | ISBN 9781608641222 ()
Classification: LCC PS3574.A85 A6 2016 (print) | LCC PS3574.A85 (ebook) | DDC
811/.54--dc23
LC record available at http://lccn.loc.gov/2016013826

Dedicated to survivors everywhere

Contents

"You can't possess radiance; you can only admire it."

—Elizabeth Taylor

BROKEN WINDOW

i was once one with the night—
    defiant building reaching for the cobalt sky
bright city lights
    the air crisp with defiance

now i watch as i lay in my bed
    listening from the distance
to the sounds of rubber against pavement speeding by,
    the occasional plane

jealous of the wind
    waiting for the storm

WITNESS

A stuffed clown with a happy smile
watched in silence

from the edge of the bed
brightly visible every night

as I sucked my pacifier
& my uncle thrust.

RHETORIC OF EMPIRE

I imagine him a heartbreaker, like I grew up to be,
perhaps with dark eyes and tattoos and a nefarious
persona. It is said he was Puerto Rican. In the '70s,
getting an Ecuadorian immigrant pregnant was
perhaps *boricua* blasphemy. The local *jibaras* would
not be having it. I've never heard from or seen or met
my father. Fact is there is nothing to prove this otherness.

Still, I see him when I stare at myself hard enough in
the mirror, when people ask where my freckles came
from, when I am naked being devoured by another man.
I picture him sitting somewhere on the island in his
guayabera with a small golden crucifix glistening against
the hairy chest I didn't inherit. He is probably mustached,
smoking cigarettes, waiting for his wife to make him dinner.

I wonder if he thinks of me as he watches the sun set below
the horizon, a daily reminder of the son he left behind.
Maybe he owns a guinea pig, a pet symbol of his experiment,
the nickname given to me—*El Cuy*—as an outcast child. I am
certain he has grown children, a hundred percent Taino,
untainted with Inca blood. They will claim his empire as I
continue to write bastard poems hoping to be remembered.

I would have atoned for him like the mother who cast me out
as her demon spawn and the stepfather that never welcomed
me as his own. I often dreamt of walking on a dirt road
with a suitcase and a couple of dollars heading toward the
vanishing tropical sun hoping to find a shadow of his smile.
Instead I travel from man to man, unattainable in this
journey to forgive myself for being born, creating chaos.

He does not know that I suffer from OCD or find humor in pathological doubt and self-destruction. He is oblivious to my being neglected by my own cultures because my Spanish has a different accent, clueless to these combined features which don't make me look one or the other but often confused for Mexican instead. Inevitably, I would have been abandoned once he found out I was gay as well.

There are no faded photographs, recorded phone conversations, birthday videos or online searches to link this history. The truth is tucked away in our hearts, underneath our pillows, in dreams, in letters never sent. In his absence, I have conquered my own kingdom. It is in the beauty of the stars in the night sky, the sounds of the ocean, the sweet taste of mangoes, the smell of coffee that we share this life as one.

INAPPROPRIATE

In third grade, my favorite teacher was Ms. Monahan. She was younger than all the others and too beautiful to be teaching math. I watched her explain how numbers were divided with her button nose, long eyelashes, luscious hair. Her favorite color was purple and she was everything I wanted to be when I grew up. We were

poor so that Christmas I asked my mom if she had anything I could re-gift for my arithmetic crush, especially anything lavender. She gave me a lovely sheer negligee that didn't fit her without any thought of its inappropriateness. I waited until all the other kids had left the classroom before handing her the giftwrapped

box. When she opened it, her soft eyes filled with terror. She looked at me in shock. If only I knew then what I later learned at the piers, I would have snapped my fingers and been like, "Girl, you better turn your boyfriend out with this shit right here! I got you, mama! Mmm-hmm!"

BECCA

When people talk about comfort foods
remembering childhood and family,
I often find myself trying to sell
the idea of *arroz con huevos.*
I somehow survived malnutrition
with white rice, two fried eggs and just a little salt.
In school, the rich kids would brag about:
meatloaf, mac & cheese, lasagna,
tater tots. I stayed silent and kept drawing,
hoping the teacher would skip me again.
I didn't know I was poor until I told Becca
what my favorite dish was and she
shared this with the other mean girls
I used to think were so cool. I wasn't even
worthy of gay sidekick status anymore
because I was an unfashionable
accessory—a poverty-stricken fag.
"We all know he likes huevos! But with white rice?"
My mom didn't get to stay home and bake cookies all day.
She had to work at the factory and come home
tired to put some dinner together. And yeah,
this makes me crave a familial embrace and
sleeping in Hulk Underoos.

So, Fuck You Becca!

BOY GEORGE AT PLAID, NYC, 2004

After his sage (or was it bitter?) advice
to never work for a lesbian, as we notice
others gathering around us in this lounge,
his height and British drag attitude
keeping them at bay, he asks if we would
join him outside for a fag, to indulge
in the glamour of his secondhand smoke,
my mum dying of cancer back at home,
we kindly decline, accept his free drink tickets
instead, star-struck club kids, and fabulously
make our way back out to battle the queens
on the dance floor, two karma chameleons.

JEAN-MICHEL BASQUIAT EXHIBIT, BROOKLYN MUSUEM, 2005

I was only seventeen
        the year you died of a heroin overdose.
Fab 5 Freddy read a poem
        by Langston at your memorial.
I was just a hustler at the piers
        you stared at weeks before.
I had no idea how I could have saved you
        or who Hughes was,
let alone that I would survive
        to become a self-destructive
artist like you. You had such incredible talent.
        Vibrant, violent, beautiful imagery.
I wonder if you noticed the same anger in my eyes
        that emanates from these paintings.
You might have imagined me hopeless,
        without a future.
It was only when I saw your picture on the cover
        of the newspapers that I discovered
the voyeur I had warned the other pier queens
        about was you.
They cared more that you had dated Madonna.
        You looked messy and high but
I would have still sucked you off the way she did
        and I might have only stolen an art piece
(or two) on the way out.
        Not that I would have known what to do
with them. Perhaps sold them to a trick
        to hang in his living room.
He would have thought it was some
        street artist knock off.
Years later, he would have sold it for millions.
        I would be here at this same museum

admiring the Basquiat I practically gave away
    for food or a place to crash or
some new sneakers. I wonder if you contemplated
    approaching an underage boy
for sex those times you watched me,
    if you would have fucked me on the floor mattress
on Great Jones Street,
    if I would have remained Untitled
or simply unspoken of.

MEN LIKE MY FATHER

Men like my father leave me behind to be with their children
and loved ones. A fond memory. Maybe a forgotten smile.
Sometimes perhaps they think of me and
wonder. These men like my father.

They make me feel special and often worth keeping,
fill my head with dreams of possibility and true love,
inspire the need for a warm parental embrace,
before revealing themselves to be men like my father.

They enjoy the softness of my body, my openness, my ecstasy,
my kisses, for a night, some months, a few years.
And then they vanish, return home to their spouses.
Men like my father.

MONA LISA AT THE LOUVRE, 2011

She smiled at me knowingly, matriarchal,
        smaller than I had imagined with
eyes penetrating past the climate-controlled, bulletproof
        glass meant to keep her gaze at a distance.
She knew my heartache—
        a survivor surrounded by crowds yet isolated.

I stared back into her eyes for a brief eternity the way I would
        watch you lying next to me in bed as you fell asleep.
We fit perfectly together as you held me in your arms back
        home in Albuquerque. I would listen to your heartbeat
with my one good ear as the world outside
        dissolved and faded into oblivion.

The chance for new love was everywhere and yet,
        she understood that years after our breakup
that one Facebook message from you destroyed me,
        ruined my vacation with memories
of our time spent together in Belgium.
        My own smile now ambiguous among my coupled

friends as they held hands in Versailles
        or called their partners while I silently ate escargot
wishing for someone to share it with.
        Your absence haunting me everywhere from
Notre Dame to the top of the Eiffel.
        That summer in Paris I watched lovers kiss

above bridges over the Seine River,
        men capture their moments with pictures outside
the steps of the Montpellier Cathedral.
        It reminded me of our photographs

at St. Bavo's in Ghent; how we imagined one day in our old
    age to look back at these with happiness.

I find myself just outside the Louvre entrance
    as men cruise behind me
in the park with their dicks in hand
    with only a fleeting desire to taste them.
Mona knows it is only your children I wanted to swallow.
    It is only your paintings I wanted to pose for.

But the landscape in the background
    was never meant to include skyscrapers,
only the Sandia Mountains.
    There would be much speculation
about what I actually meant to you—
    how valuable our time together really was.

Perhaps you were just another spectator
    moving on to take in another masterpiece.
I remain framed awaiting your return.

PENICILLIN

It would be my grandmother who caught syphilis—
the one I missed most while turning tricks out on the streets.

'Buelo had been a womanizer, left her infected.
She moved to this country already plagued with disease—

never sought treatment out of shame or gave herself to another as I
devoured enough to make up for both (and

more). The truth came out as she was going blind.
I bought her fishnet stockings and condoms for Christmas.

I wonder if she ever expected her grandson to be the whore she
feared being called.

IF SOMEBODY WERE TO BREAK INTO MY APARTMENT

and go through my DVR recordings, they would mistakenly
assume a fifteen-year-old girl lives there. They might play

with my cute and cuddly cat and go into a drawer to find some
basic makeup. They might be compelled to watch old

episodes of *Vampire Diaries* and lust over the entire cast of studs,
the Salvatore brothers, Damon and Stefan, but

mostly (my favorite) younger brother Jeremy (hit pause on him
shirtless!). Based on a young adult series, written by an

author who must own a VHS copy of *Pretty in Pink* somewhere in
her fancy house, this is the standard girl-gets-

chased-by-multiple-suitors' storyline but with vampires,
werewolves and witches. It is a known fact that the fantasy

of every teenage girl (and gay boy) is to have multiple options to
choose from to spend eternity with forever (and

ever). (And, yes, I believe Andy should have ended up with
Duckie.) I can't speak for girls that mature to become

women but most boys that grow up to be gay would simply bang
the shit out of all of them, and probably at the same

time, in one glorious supernatural orgy. Not everyone wants to be
married or gay married and so they could all end up

living happily ever after in some polyamorous or open relationship
and continue to sleep with one another like

they do on these shows anyway. Between *Arrow* and *The Flash*, if I
ever found myself on a CW set, I would have

no shame being a tramp. I suppose these criminals might also be
thrown off by my recordings of *New Girl, 2Broke Girls*

and *Girls*. Maybe they would enjoy hours of MTV's *Teen Wolf,*
where I agree with little sluts everywhere that Tyler Posey

and, especially, Dylan O'Brien are worth howling at the moon over.
They might question why I still watch *The Simpsons* or

still have unwatched episodes of (now cancelled) *Glee*. After going
through my DVR, they might look under my bed where

they would find a selection of wigs and think I like
to play dress up a lot, maybe try one on for fun. They would scour

through my bookshelf and note all the chick lit like
Jane Eyre, The Fault in Our Stars and *Eat Pray Love*. Maybe

they would think I'm suicidal and take pity on me with all the
Sylvia Plath and Virginia Woolf collections. And then they would

open up the bottom drawer next to my bed and
discover the leather mask and harness and dildo.

WORKING AT THE PUBLISHING HOUSE IN NY

Surrounded by books that will be read by more people than all of my small press poetry collections combined. Amused but not encouraged by the children's book on my shelf about the farting dog and my idea of writing a spoof called *Scat in the Hat*—a one-page board book where the only words (after the cat takes off his hat) would be "Oh, shit!" My *Fifty Shades of Grey* trilogy box set mocking me for a far more deviant sex life. Difficult to feel inspired in this small cubicle outside the boss's office, on a dark lonely corner with no sunlight (except for when she leaves her door open). A far cry from the club kid days when I could get by on three hours sleep after partying all night at the discotheque. A coworker asks if I could request a new ISBN for a premium book project. "Sure thing!" I say (I've learned never to admit if I'm drowning). It's putting together and editing our catalogs that I've come to love. The smart-ass mailroom guy asks for my autograph and leaves behind boxes of new galleys for me to distribute. I keep my iPhone near. I go back to the photograph you just sent me, the one of you at a beautiful beach in Sicily. This passion is now yours, and I'm waiting to kiss you again; I imagine myself swimming ashore in Italy to be with you.

BELLUM SACRUM

Every life is valuable but, unlike the throats of boys bruised
with handprints, not if taken with distant rockets.

Religion is seemingly a punch(line) in the art of war.
Casualties are just images in the news unless

corpses weigh you down. In search for safe spaces, fingers
wedge into earth that becomes self-made graves. All

those insides spilled outside look no different against the soil.
If you taste their blood, regardless of skin or who was

worshipped with breath, it is likely all the same. It is difficult to
gauge the wisdom of time bringing things into

clearer perspective when the same mistakes are made over and
over (and yet over) again. Revenge is bringing

criminals to justice, not collective punishment, not collateral
damage—civilians, families, the newly murdered are

more full of life than memory. Light darkens in front of the eyes of
children as death becomes homeland.

Whatever God is prayed to will not take sides from bleachers or
hold up a scoreboard. The prophets are stuck in

an ambulance stalled in the middle of bombed out roads. This land
below stars—birthplace of religions with the

concept of heaven—is furthest from holy.

THE RECOVERING ADDICT AND THE HATE CRIME SURVIVOR

When he joked

about his meth mouth
to make light

of his drug addiction and fucked-up teeth,

I smiled
if only to look amused

Still, I wanted to kiss him

instead I showed him
the scar on the back of my head

told him I hadn't heard

a single word he said
with my deaf ear

and our moment passed

AN IDEAL HUSBAND

"To love oneself is the beginning of a lifelong romance."

—Oscar Wilde

I will paint my face white and become a Virgin Queen. This is all I
have left to look forward to in life. This is the wisdom of

retired prostitutes and failed poets alike. There needs not be a
lingering fatal disease or obvious signs of aging for one to

accept the fact that all sacrifices have led to this. The Art you so
adamantly thought valuable above all else, appreciated as

mediocre, manifests as the empty space next to you at the poetry
reading, in bed, in the park feeding squirrels.

Death is a heart that takes forever to heal and does not welcome.
Memories are lost when shared with cats, the wind,

the open sky, the stars at night. Our Lady Madonna once said, *"Life
is a mystery / Everyone must stand alone"* but in the

version laid out here nothing follows but silence. No choir. An
abandoned church where the statues do not come alive or

dance. Much like wealthy scholars, all they do is watch. And judge.
Perhaps take pity on your soul. The flame from the

candle struggling to survive knowing that once it goes out it will be
replaced. I only loved the unattainable, believed in

promises far-fetched—the gift of missing fathers. Disney is not to
blame. Princess stories were not meant for boys who

played with dolls. Neither are *telenovelas* accountable for that
matter. All this drama is your reality show. *"You are*

trouble!" were the words of your last possible suitor over dinner
with friends. Maybe he meant *"troubled."* Playing with

the dessert seemed more fitting than arguing with another writer.
His world will continue on without you and soon

enough he too will marry, apply for grants and win awards. Going
through all your rejection letters is a great way to pass

the time during the weekend. So is looking through pictures of
your ex with his new boyfriend on Facebook and

Instagram. Sometimes you just have to accept that this is what you
were meant for. Passion is overrated. You might die

writing words that will never be read.

SWEET DREAMS

He calls to wish me sweet dreams, the wall above his bed featuring
Van Gogh's *Starry Night*. Jealousy over his new

boyfriend is a tropical storm that came out of nowhere over my
weathered heart. This after sharing intimate details

about their sex life over the phone as I imagine myself in an open
field waiting for him naked under sunshine with wet

grass at my feet—the closest I will ever feel to his tongue against
my skin. He cannot detect the bitterness in my voice

growling at him like a wild animal in heat. When he shared this
bed with me, I might as well have slept alone in the

middle of a forest fire. At least then I could feel the burn. We hang
up and I expect to hear silence but, instead, it is the roar of

motorcycles and the New York City skyline
lit up in the distance.

ANONYMOUS

This is not a place to fall in love.
It is dark and hunger prevails.
You will not be the first,
likely not the last. I didn't come here
for that. In the outside world,
we could have been a couple.
I only need to fill a void,
just temporary intimacy.

Don't ask any questions.
I lie and live in the moment.
Relax. Forget that this mouth
is famous. These hands hold
more than pens.
You came for this—
to be desired and let go.
I taste it on your skin.

It is in the way you watch
from above with ecstasy.
Pretend I am yours forever—
to cherish, to hold, to fuck.
There are no stories here.
Nobody that comes is worthy
yet everyone has a reason.
Just don't let them touch

without permission. Monsters
tend to troll for weakness. It is
all they have left in this world.
We can still escape.
There are beds more comfortable

with partners that have names.
Someone who buys our innocence.
Soft pillows to dream upon.

This feeling cannot last forever
but it can be remembered.

RED

Every one you have ever truly been in love with
Every moment you have feared for your life,
something punishable by law or a society of oppression

Every time you wanted to scream,
to hold him or her in your arms
to protect them from the world around you

Same is two becoming one
that one love that is the same love
the sameness of two in love

Born free and then told who to be
shaped to fill
an acceptable mold

Your heart belongs to them
Your heart must be controlled
Your heart is not your own

Love is what they determine
Love is what they preach
and love is why they destroy

Children must not be exposed
Christ will not return as long
as *they* continue to love

Pain and suffering
will not end
until *they* do

It is time for *them* to die
It is time for demons to retreat
It is time for humiliation

Russia—I have fallen in love with your beautiful men
muscular   feeding hunger   hardworking fathers
watching sunsets   learning cultures   drinks   music

Russia—I imagined myself a lover   lost   in your language
a wardrobe of coats   a warm embrace against my body
searching for translations of poetry and lineage of history

I too have survived by remaining distant and misunderstood
the villainous, untrustworthy spy
thoughts of socialism and a radical too

My Russian lover in America holds my hand
on the subway all the way from Brighton Beach
because he can and does not care that people stare

He knows that even here we could be killed
unwelcome to appear as anything more than
two men traveling together, no PDA allowed

A Russian man guns us down with his eyes
Back home, our body bags would be spit upon
shame that someone from his country has been tainted

not even by an American per se, a minority of Latino descent
all we share in common is being other
left to the fringes of distant cities

raised to believe in sin and documentation
rent   bills   procreation
devastation   government

It is only winters that we understand
harsh winds
hats   gloves

I have been beaten by strangers,
my own kind, non-Soviet,
on our own pavements

I have been left out in the cold
for dead to go to hell
without bus fare

the same moon that shines in all countries—my guidance
shining bright for all sisters and brothers
regardless of what is deemed natural or unnatural

offering light to darkness and predators
how do we boycott the sun?
How many wars must be waged?

When do damaged children find salvation?
Is this same love a new thing to the world?
Can all those who think differently be destroyed?

none of it is anything new
none of it has been contained
if spirits walk the earth, then some of them have loved too

and heaven   perhaps   is crowded
with dead lovers   odd aunts   strange uncles
with men and boobies   women confused for boys

and loneliness   but mostly   want
and struggle   seemingly   only belongs
to color   religion   race   creed   politics

countries of angry teens
countries of guns and altars
a country of men

where will the perverts be buried?
when will *they* stop being born?
why do *they* plague every corner of the earth?

on this day it is the loved
and loving that must bleed
and those who speak openly about love

they will turn the sky red
after *they* are gone
the world will be the same

BRITTLE

You meet him at the club.
He is Chinese and Australian
with an indiscernible accent.
Beautiful muscle toned body.
Tall with blue eyes and Asian features.
A total hottie. You take him back
to your Bushwick apartment.
The sex is fantastic. His cock is heaven.
You find yourself in Kama Sutra–like poses.
You had no idea you could be so flexible.
He leaves you exhausticated.
He spends the night and takes you out
to breakfast at one of those trendy hipster
spots in your own hood.
You hook up again a couple of more times but
he is getting attached very quickly.
He starts referring to you as his man and
his boyfriend when you've only welcomed
him in as your boy toy.
You consider the possibilities and gorgeous
children you could never have.
Your friends would love him and be
happy you're settled.
It just seems too damn amazing but you say
"What the fuck!" and get to know him better.
And then you find out it is.

He works at a nail salon.

In New Jersey.

what we choose to remember
what we choose to forget

a new drug known as crack appeared on the streets
the same year
Venus Xtravaganza, 23, was found strangled under a bed in
a hotel room (four days after her death)

South Africa freed Nelson Mandela
the same year
Julio Rivera was murdered in NYC by two men who beat him
with a hammer & stabbed him with a knife for being gay

Tupac Shakur was gunned down
the same year
Nick Moraida, 37, was killed by a member of the Aryan
Brotherhood, posing as a male prostitute during an
attempted robbery

the Twin Towers collapsed on 9/11
the same year
Fred Martinez, Jr., 16, a Navajo two spirit student, was
bludgeoned to death in Colorado because he was a "fag"

Eminem won at the MTV Awards
the same year
Gwen Araujo, 17, was beaten and strangled by four men in
Newark, California

Hurricane Katrina hit and Pope John Paul II died
the same year
James Maestas, 21, was assaulted outside a Santa Fe

restaurant and followed to a hotel where he was beaten unconscious

a student went on a killing spree at Virginia Tech and Apple introduced the iPhone
the same year
Ruby Ordeñana, 24, a transgender woman was found naked and strangled in San Francisco

Fidel Castro stepped down as President of Cuba and writers went on strike in Hollywood
the same year
Lawrence King, 15, was shot and killed in school by 14-year-old Brandon because he was effeminate and flamboyant

Michael Jackson and Farrah Fawcett died and a plane landed on the Hudson River
the same year
Jorge Stevens Lopez Mercado, 19, a gay rights advocate, was found decapitated, dismembered and partially burned in Puerto Rico

Haiti was devastated by an earthquake
the same year
Amanda Gonzalez-Andujar, 29, a trans woman was strangled and doused with bleach in her Queens apartment and Ashley Santiago, another trans woman, was found naked and stabbed fourteen times in the kitchen of her home

Osama Bin Laden was finally killed and Don't Ask, Don't Tell was officially repealed
the same year
Rosita Hernandez, a Cuban trans woman was stabbed to death in Miami and Camila Guzman, a transgender woman was found murdered in her East Harlem apartment

a gunman opened fire during a screening of *The Dark Knight* in
Aurora, Colorado and Hurricane Sandy hit
the same year
*Kyra Cordova, 27, a trans woman was found dead in the
woods of Philadelphia*

mariposas/brown lives/queer lives/trans lives
we fly in our dreams
brighten skies
still know the sun for flight
the wind for guidance
yet sometimes we're invisible

may our souls linger over fields/prayers
our names/stories remind them
we are worth love
know god

There is beauty in darkness, in the night sky,
in the eyes of *mi gente*
Beautiful is our love
Splendid is our survival
Our history is sacred and worth remembering

TRIBUTE TO ANGEL, HALLOWEEN, 2014

In an interview with the *Huffington Post,* Michael Alig insists that you were family in spite of how much fun they made of you and your clothes and called you a wannabe. He talks a lot about how you were similarly disenfranchised and he loved you, no matter how badly things ended—your body chopped up and tossed into the river. He wants to help runaway youth and thinks he could be a better role model because of what he has experienced.

As I walk down the streets in my platform shoes with my naval officer hat, angel wings and harness, people stop to take my photograph and excitedly announce that they know who I am supposed to be. As if they had just won a lottery because they remember hearing about your gruesome murder back in the '90s or watched Wilson Cruz play a decidedly Hollywood version of who you really were in *Party Monster*.

The week before you went missing, as I threw out the garbage from my West Village apartment, we finally made peace while discussing the death of New York City nightlife thanks to Mayor Giuliani. Little did we know that it would be your actual murder that would destroy what was left of gay club culture. You were sweet and seemed kind and, yes, I too mocked you for your sense of fashion. As if I knew any better in my banjee gear with clipped eyebrows and baggy jeans. We were young. We were shady bitches but we pier queens looked out for one another.

It is drizzling outside much like the last night I saw you alive. The feathers on my angel wings will smell like a poultry shop by the time I get to the train station. The L train, like the Limelight, is filled with costumed partiers who just want to be in their beds with their pets or loved ones or families or tricks for the night.

You don't get to go home and I wonder where Michael sleeps tonight. I want to show up at his doorstep dressed like you—fully alive with hammer in hand.

ÁRBOL

There came a day when it was
decided it was time for you to be cut
down. And so they pulled you apart,
destroyed your bark for sharing
truths. They took one of your roots
and left you scarred for life. A life
that would continue. When they
noticed you stood your ground and
again survived, the forest mocked
and discredited you. Your soul cried
out. But your resilience was never
taken into account. Instead, the rain
washed away your fears, cleansed
your wounds with her delicate touch.
Pink flowers blossomed from your
stems in spite of lack of light and
infertile soil. And as you grew taller
and left them behind, the sun glowed
bigger and brighter bursting from
the sky and birds settled onto your
branches. You nurtured their
passion, provided comfortable
retreat. Your journey out into
the world would be their stories.

GENTRIFICATION

This is the dust of dreams that once prevailed. Displaced bohemian
memories erased for the sake of high value. Us who created
something from nothing to make it appealing

for those who own everything. We who were poor before it
was trendy to sport the look of struggle. The three-story building in
which I chose to stay is now gutted. Leaving me

to fight from the top of a treehouse with nothing below. A siege of
hipsters await outside armed with PBR cans and
artisanal mayo while our people are scattered throughout

dangerous lands they do not know. Once homeless, the
guerilla tactics of moral disintegration remain futile toward

me. Even then I battled for my house—dance floors similarly
held by beams and joists. I remain in this ghost town with my
ancestors watching hipsters skateboard down the street

in grandpa clothes unaware they soon will be the disenfranchised
and undesirable. This is the sound of the world changing.

SQUATTER

There was a large spider I named Sasha
    that spun his web daily
in front of my entrance door.

The only thing he ever caught in his silk was me.
    He was determined. Refused to believe I had dreams.
His design was spectacular. Sasha waited patiently for the
    day he could poison and paralyze my ambition.

One day he just disappeared.
    Nothing left behind but a memory.

I still look for him before I put in the key.
    Afraid he will jump out of nowhere.
I actually miss him now. Wonder where he is and
    what other insects he may find along the way.

I DON'T REALLY CARE

that my mother calls to
announce she is
officially heartbroken. Again.
Her daily dramatic *telenovela*
moments have made her something
of a joke within the
family. Even my *abuela*
doesn't like to answer
the phone when she reaches
out anymore. It is
always some awful
dream that she believes to be
profound with meaning or
the untimely death of
a ninety-year-old elder. She makes
herself out to have been
the closest friend of
some unknown stranger or
distant relative that passed
away unexpectedly
to something like cancer.
No te acuerdas de Sebastian?
I have no
recollection of ever
meeting this person.
She insists that
he was a big part of my
childhood. She is going
to send flowers, light some
candles to all of her saints
and pray for his soul. She
might have met him once at a

dinner party or he
might be a friend's husband's third
cousin. I am sorry for
his death but know
the family
probably doesn't even
know who she is. My mom
is devastated and does not
know why life can be so cruel.
There must be a way she can
attend the funeral. My
eyes roll. She thrives on this
suffering. Watching the news is
her drug. Not a day goes by sans
misery. I tell her
in Spanish that
she never really lived because
her entire life has been the
fear of death. She is
silent. There is nothing but
a ghost on the other side of
the phone.

MUNDANE

We don't always have the time
to truly listen to stories, clip our nails,
nap with pets, enjoy our meals.
But it is in these rare moments
that we get a little closer to life.

U R

For Brian

Eres the sweet belly offering of my cat
  I am unafraid to rub even with his claws out.

Eres the Mexican blanket and tube socks that keep me warm
  as I listen to the winter winds howling outside my corner
Bushwick apartment.

Eres the candle I light when the electricity goes out—
  offering hope in the darkness throughout the city night.

Eres the Listerine strip that keeps me confident with minty kisses,
  fresh breath and perhaps even more
(if I end up on my knees).

Eres the cookies & cream ice cream at the end of a long day
  that I like to spoon around to slightly melt before eating in
front of the TV.

Eres the sheet fort built as a child to enjoy my own little world—
  keeping me safe on the living room sofa bed
from arguing parents in the bedroom.

Eres the chocolates found inside a plastic pumpkin pail on
  Halloween.

Eres the reassuring touch of *abuela's* wrinkled soft hand.

Eres the bobble head Jesus with outstretched hands that holds my
  writer's pen.

Eres my favorite feather pillow that I like to squoosh and fall
  asleep on to dream.

FOR COLORED BOYS WHO HAVE BEEN CONSIDERED CRIMINALS

All I wanted was to catch the 6 p.m. ferry.
My boyfriend would have driven me back
to Bushwick but why make him go out of his way.
It was only a ferry and subway ride and I had
Madonna's *Rebel Heart* to listen to.
The right headphone used only as a prop.
All my life I have been some sort of victim.
I've been used to racing.
Little gay boys learn to speed
at an early age to survive from bullies.
Ten years ago, they finally caught up to me and left
me with this subtle handicap—
complete deafness in my right ear.
I failed to hear him as he singled me out.
I could have been ignoring him.
I could have been trying to escape.
I could have been resisting arrest.
I know the story I could have become had I
not finally heard the barking.
I didn't think about all the colored boys
shot and killed for running away from the police.
I wasn't fazed by the crowd gathering to
find out what was going on.
When he asked to check my bag,
I naturally started to open it.
I didn't realize I could have been gunned
down for following instinct—
his hand on the holster ready to pull the gun out.
I was yelled at to stop and place my bag on the
floor for the police dog to sniff.
I only thought this creature was adorable—
beautiful sable black like my cat.
It happened so fast.

No drugs or weapons of mass destruction
or rainbow colored Skittles.
What I did have was about as many spectators
as I would at a poetry event.
That was it. I immediately lost myself
in the crowd as the doors opened to let us aboard.
The whole ride back, I spent considering
the statistic I could have been.
Wondering if I had looked like I didn't belong.
As a child it was if I laughed too loud
or waved my hands too much
or wore clothes that were too bright.
As an adult it is if I look threatening
or suspicious
or dress like a thug.
In a moment, it could have all escalated
to a morning news headline.
All they saw was someone who
could breathe and had two ears.
Others have died because sometimes blue
only sees black or brown.
Books are judged by their covers.
Poems are not often read between the lines.
There is no time for nuance or noticing disability
or illness or struggle.
Had I been a white woman
with a Louis Vuitton bag, I would not have been asked,
perhaps even ushered through.
I know the horror of the world we live in.
I know the fear being myself can cause.
I know the blood I could have shed (same).
I know the lives that have been lost.
I know the mothers that have cried.
I know the loved ones left behind.
I know sometimes it only takes a moment.
I know sometimes it only takes the wrong move.

HIPSTER

You've likely mistaken me for some old-school native Latino. But
gringo, I know how to read and I'm not just talking literature.
Allow me to flip that crochet hat nestled upon your unwashed hair.
Your beards, ironic T-shirts, Variety coffee cups and thrift shop
hand-me-downs fail to

impress this anchor baby. Your legacy will end much like ours once
the yuppie parents move into the nabe. Unaffordable rents and
no regard for your cultural contributions will plague you too. You
will know what it is like to be considered roaches that need to be
pushed out.

Those roommates—friends-for-life—will think of you fondly
like dead goldfish flushed down the toilet. Their parents will gladly
take them back and listen to their stories of "struggle" in the hood.
Their art possibly forgotten, their accents parodied, their fashion
so two thousand and yesterday. You

will have to settle for being ignored, looked down upon,
felt pity for by the new conquerors. This undesirable dismissal
should actually be considered kindness. Perhaps embrace the circle
of life. It's nothing you can't survive as you mature from insolence
and nothing looking back at the

absurdity of man buns and skinny jeans won't someday heal. You'll
soon realize it was never about talent or privilege but all about
money in the end. Hopefully you saved some benjamins but it's
certain mommy and daddy will bail you out. It's just the world we
live in and things

change.

BESIDE MYSELF

Yes, worry. Your time has come and gone.
There was a time you were beautiful.
You've become the father you never met.
Like how Christians assume they know Jesus
though he looks nothing like they imagine.
You are not going to be remembered.
The best thing you ever did was keep a cat
alive for over sixteen years.
All you have is that rent-stabilized apartment
with the cracked paint and broken windows.
You'll get over it. No one ever expected this
much from you anyway. You should've died
a long time ago. You're lucky. There's a man
who loves you in spite of your age and failure.
& you can still have a future, as the winter
season approaches, with someone who will
keep you warm at night and fill you up inside.
Your body may not be what it used to but
it can continue to provide pleasure.
You reinvented yourself many times before
& your mouth yet has stories to share.
Let go of the past, the revolution has fresh
faces at the forefront. Move on. Your words
can no longer signal change. & opening doors
does not mean you get to stay in the room. It
gets crowded very quickly. You become invisible
like the dead poets before you. Finish your drink
and grab an hors d'oeuvre before you go. Perhaps
outside it is cold & blustery but, you'll see, that thick
skin will come in quite handy.

WHEN YOUR DOCTOR CALLS TO TELL YOU THAT YOUR BRAIN TUMOR IS BACK

respond quietly in the car so as not to alarm
your boyfriend, your mother, your aunt.
try not to react as you sit in traffic
and he tries to convince you not to worry.

be grateful you are not the one driving
as the world outside collapses and the song
on the satellite radio fades into the distance.

tune out and remember the terrible surgery,
the weeks with a partially paralyzed face,
the cane in your closet needed to get around
the Bushwick apartment you fought to stay in.

don't reveal your fear over the phone of the risk
of living the rest of your life looking like a stroke
victim. don't be sad at the thought of not surviving
this after everything you've already been through.

focus on the people walking by oblivious to
the fact it's only been nine years (a symbolic
number for you) since you woke up with your
head bandaged and fragile happy to be alive.

when he hangs up, note the silent anticipation.
you could lie and say it was a wrong number.
your mother will just continue complaining
about her problems from the backseat.

you could change the station and ask everyone
where they would like to go eat. how much time
do you have left to live? what happens now?

say it out loud and, whatever you do, don't cry.
be real and tell them that we're all going
to die someday. you've always known life is short
and lived it to the fullest with no regrets.

truth is you never expected to live this long. this
will just be something else to write about. boys
like us are never meant to get an uncomplicated ending.

we ride across the bridge deep in thought (or shock)
as the city disappears behind us with our laughter.
this is a new journey and we don't know where
we're heading. i want to be a handsome corpse.

i will let this grow inside of me. maybe i'll name it.
i couldn't bear another ugly scar. in my head, with
this uninvited guest, all i might believe is that i have
lived and loved and still have time to change the world.

SCHWANNOMA

In my head I have a benign tumor with a name that sounds like
something you order at a Mediterranean restaurant.

Unfortunately, whether the size of a pea or a meatball, I can't eat it
like everything else. I want to give it a drag queen

name—something fierce and funny like Shenani Gans or Jenny C.
Qua. If my hair falls out after radiation, I could

wear headscarves and walk around in my apartment as I recover in
skimpy outfits so I could become my dream female

impersonator—Little Edie Chacon. I'd have to make a video doing
a sexy Puerto Rican freak flag dance unless I end up

laid out in bed with my cat feeling more like Big Iris. I'm not quite
sure what fate this abnormal growth has in store for

me but I'll be picking myself back up from this death drop.
Sometimes laughter helps you persevere, not to mention

white dancing shoes.

PREPARATIONS

I prepare for radiation
like planning for a weekend getaway
wondering what I will wear,
when to make time for naps.

I buy enough cat food and litter
to make sure my cat is taken care of
wondering if we will cuddle
when I return home.

I prepare for radiation
like planning for a weekend getaway
checking weather reports and setting
aside comfortable clothes for the trip ahead.

RADIANCE

For Brian

You will take care of me after radiation. I will appear to be perfectly fine and still make you cackle with my humor and wit. We will go see a Broadway show the next evening for the holidays and then we will enjoy a heavy dinner which will make me wish my appetite had been suppressed. I'll make catty comments about the clientele. I will make you forget the bandages just came off that morning. My new fancy hat will conceal the wounds. I'll let you complain about your friends and browse through Facebook to see who got married and who just had another baby. And the next day we'll celebrate

Christmas and gift each other with the latest Apple technology. We'll go to my mom's to be with my family before the two-hour drive to your sister's in Connecticut. The memories of nails driven into my skull will dissipate in

fear of a deer jumping out at us on the road. Speed limits will help gauge recovery time. When we arrive, Duke the dog will substitute for Alexis the cat and the love that healed breakups and violent attacks and surgery. There will be no time to think about headaches or nausea or tiredness. In fact, there will be no symptoms out of the ordinary other than an early

night. You will perhaps be more exhausted emotionally than I am physically. We'll come back to my apartment in time to put together a last-minute New Year's Eve party much like I had originally hoped to have before the diagnosis. There will be family and close friends and lots of Fireball shots, of course. I will laugh at your imitations of the local hipsters and kiss you when the ball drops in Times Square. By then, my bruises will look like nothing more than chickenpox. We will have better sex than most healthy, younger couples.

It'll be like nothing ever happened except for the selfie I took of myself while drugged up wearing a metal piece on my head. The two of us simply happy that we found each other after all these years.

BEACON FALLS

Winter, a cul-de-sac, an Xbox 360, and a holiday cookie swap—
a suitable recovery after radiation
to explore suburbia: an escape from city life,
a small town located a few minutes from Sandy Hook
where neighbors still collect guns, children trained in case of
another mental illness breakdown emergency.
Something sinks in—the fact that others your age
are married (or divorced) with children—a world different from the
club scenes and museums you are used to,
those family television shows making sense after all these years.
You finally understand why your parents spent
so much time in front of that large tube, eventual flat screen with
surround-sound system: always on in the background,
one in every room, the soundtrack for all occasions. For you, this
was not the real world. For them, it was the American dream.
Out here, men secretly cheat on their wives; soccer moms with
masculine haircuts and coffee cups spiked with alcohol ring cow
bells—focusing on children's sports games and each other. In the
backyards, wild animals behave like wild animals, without regret,
in the quiet darkness. Few locals look like you but sometimes
pass through. Malls are tourist attractions: chain restaurants and
several liquor stores, everyone knows everybody's business,
outcasts are not invited to holiday house parties, outside
it is cold but the homes are always kept warm.

GROUNDHOG DAY, 2016

It is raining outside in Bushwick tonight
& my boyfriend is miles away in Staten Island.
The new floor tiles in the hallway slowly dry
as my great uncle quietly fades at a hospice in the Bronx.
I feel him take his last breath:
the flames from the boiler signal
time for his cremation.
Ashes is what he wished to become.
The family suffers and all I
could fathom is a nap. Death,
unlikely ally, here I rest my head
upon these flattened pillows. It is time.
It is time I allowed myself
the privilege of getting sick.

ABOUT THE AUTHOR

Emanuel Xavier, an LGBT History Month Icon, is author of the poetry collections *Nefarious, Americano: Growing up Gay and Latino in the USA, Pier Queen, If Jesus Were Gay & other poems*, and the novel *Christ Like*. He also edited *Mariposas: A Modern Anthology of Queer Latino Poetry, Bullets & Butterflies: Queer Spoken Word Poetry*, and *Me No Habla with Acento: Contemporary Latino Poetry*. His work also appears in the books *For Colored Boys Who Have Considered Suicide When the Rainbow is Still Not Enough, Born This Way: Real Stories of Growing Up Gay* and *Untangling the Knot—Queer Voices on Marriage, Relationships & Identity*. He is recipient of a NYC Council Citation and has been a finalist for Lambda Literary Awards and International Latino Books Awards.

A victim of sexual abuse, a former homeless gay teen, street hustler and drug dealer, and eventual hate crime survivor, his often narrative poetry features political, sexual, and religious themes which continue to inspire new generations of confessional poetry. One of the first openly gay Nuyorican poets, he has been a longtime gay rights activist, AIDS activist and homeless youth advocate. He has spoken at The United Nations as part of The International Symposium on Cultural Diplomacy in the USA, was a featured TEDx speaker and was filmed for a documentary on poets from around the world. He continues to perform at colleges and universities throughout the country and his books are often included in LGBT and Latino Studies courses.

Other Books by Emanuel Xavier

978-1-60864-073-7

Pier Queen

978-1-60864-074-4

Americano

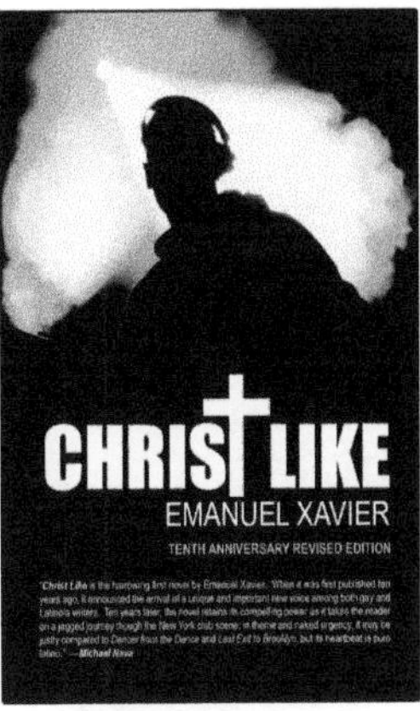

978-1-097908-385-3

Christ Like

978-1-60864-094-2

Nefarious

978-1-60864-032-4

If Jesus Were Gay
& other poems

978-1-60864-039-3

Me No Habla
With Acento
Edited by Emanuel Xavier

REBEL
SATORI
PRESS

WWW.REBELSATORIPRESS.COM

www.ingramcontent.com/pod-product-compliance
Ingram Content Group UK Ltd.
Pitfield, Milton Keynes, MK11 3LW, UK
UKHW020416250726
13967UKWH00007B/2667

9 781608 641215